Plants of Christmas

Plants of Christmas

by Hal Borland

Paintings by
Anne Ophelia Dowden

Thomas Y. Crowell
New York

Plants of Christmas
Text copyright © 1969, 1987 by Hal Borland
Illustrations copyright © 1969 by Anne Ophelia Dowden
All rights reserved. No part of this book
may be used or reproduced in any manner
whatsoever without written permission
except in the case of brief quotations
embodied in critical articles and reviews.
Printed in the United States of America.
For information address Thomas Y. Crowell Junior Books,
10 East 53rd Street, New York, N.Y. 10022.
Published simultaneously in Canada by
Fitzhenry & Whiteside Limited, Toronto.

The material in this book was adapted
from an original article in Audubon *magazine.*

Library of Congress Cataloging-in-Publication Data
Borland, Hal, 1900–1978.
  Plants of Christmas.

  Summary: Explores the legends and symbols of the
traditional plants of Christmas, such as English holly,
ivy, mistletoe, and poinsettia.
  1. Christmas decorations—Juvenile literature.
2. Plants—Folklore—Juvenile literature. [1. Plants—
Folklore. 2. Christmas decorations] I. Dowden, Anne
Ophelia Todd, 1907–   , ill. II. Title.
GT4988.B67 1987   398'.368   87-552
ISBN 0-690-04649-9
ISBN 0-690-04650-2 (lib. bdg.)

1 2 3 4 5 6 7 8 9 10
Revised Edition

Contents

POINSETTIA—*Euphorbia pulcherrima*
DOUGLAS FIR—*Pseudotsuga menziesii*
GLASTONBURY THORN—*Crataegus monogyna*
ENGLISH HOLLY—*Ilex aquifolium*
CLUB MOSS—*Lycopodium complanatum*
CHRISTMAS ROSE—*Helleborus niger*
AMERICAN MISTLETOE—*Phoradendron flavescens*

Introduction

The celebration of Christmas, which has been called "the festival of all festivals," is for Americans today a composite of traditions from many lands and many eras. Long ago, with the coming of Christianity, people all over the world dedicated the plants they knew and loved to the Holy Family. Thus our traditional Christmas includes customs from early Greece, ancient Rome, the Near East, druid Britain, Germany, and the Norse countries.

Some of our most colorful Christmas customs originated in the forested northland of Europe—the Christmas tree, the Yule log, the carols. Many of these customs were included in the tradition that the English colonists first brought to America. Later, groups from other parts of the world brought their own lore, and America itself added the turkey and the poinsettia.

In all these Christmas celebrations, plants have been important both as symbols and as decorations. Most of them were plants that people knew well. Some had long traditions of supernatural virtues, some were valued for their healing powers, and many were items of everyday use in the form of fuel or tools, food or building material.

These plants of Christmas were not suggested by the Bible itself. In the accounts of the birth of Christ, there is no mention of any plant, with the possible exception of the gifts presented by the Magi—frankincense and myrrh were precious fragrant resins from Asiatic trees.

Since most of these Christmas customs and legends are European in origin, the plants pictured in the following *pages are the original European species, some of which now grow commonly in the United States. However, our Christmas bouquet is partly American: Its Douglas fir is a New World conifer, its American mistletoe is a different species from the one the ancient druids gathered, and its poinsettia was quite unknown to Christians before Spanish missionaries came to Mexico.*

Glastonbury Thorn

Crataegus monogyna

The Glastonbury thorn
is a common English hawthorn,
but legend says this particular tree
at Glastonbury Abbey grew
from a staff Joseph of Arimathea thrust into the soil
when he arrived to Christianize England.
It thrived and came to bloom on Christmas,
and trees grown from its cuttings were believed to heal
all who touched them on Christmas day.
In Elizabethan times a Puritan who tried to destroy
the parent tree cut one of its twin trunks
but was blinded by its thorns as it fell.
Glastonbury thorns continued to bloom at Christmas
until 1752, when England adopted
the Gregorian calendar. The change shifted
the date of Christmas by eleven days,
and when the famous thorn failed to bloom
on the new Christmas there was brief rebellion
against the new calendar.

1

Sainfoin

Onobrychis viciifolia

Lady's Bedstraw

Galium verum

Legends say that much of the hay in the manger
on the night of the Nativity
came to bloom in celebration. Among the
legendary plants was sainfoin, a European legume
related to the vetches, with spikes of pink flowers.
It is supposed to have formed a wreath around the
head of the Babe. The common name, sainfoin, means
wholesome hay, not holy hay as is sometimes said.
Also in the stable's legendary hay was lady's bedstraw,
a member of a family of weeds common in America
and often called cleavers.
In Europe it was used to stuff mattresses
because it was supposed to repel fleas.
The legends say Mary lay on a bed of this bedstraw
and that when Jesus was born, it burst into yellow bloom.
For this it was rewarded with golden flowers,
though most bedstraws have white flowers.

Norway Spruce

Picea abies

The evergreen tree usually is called a fir in the legends
because "fir" is the layman's term for all evergreens
and because few of those who translated the legends
knew botany. In most cases
the tree probably was the Norway spruce,
which was king of the conifer forests.
In England it was symbolic of life enduring.
In Germany it was decorated with lights,
flowers, and colored eggs. Harz Mountain girls
danced around the decorated tree and held an imp
captive there until he provided gifts for them.
One legend says the "fir" was the original
Tree of Life in Eden and had big leaves and blossoms
until Eve ate of its fruit. In punishment, its leaves
were shrunken to needles, its fruit to cones.
Another legend says it bloomed again
the night of the Nativity
and thus became the first Christmas tree.

Oak

Quercus robur

The oak is perhaps the most widely respected
of all trees. Jews, Greeks, and Romans considered it
sacred, and the Celts
dedicated it to their gods of thunder and fire.
Oaks were preeminent among forest trees
of northern Europe, symbols of strength
and immortality—so holy that
they even imparted special value to plants that grew
on them, such as mistletoe.
Throughout most of Europe, the Yule logs
kindled on Christmas Eve were always oak.
This custom is as old as the ancient druids, who
declared that at the time of the Yule
festival all fires must be extinguished and
then relighted from the druids' sacred flame.
Quite apart from its legendary virtues,
the oak is an extremely valuable tree.
Its hard, tough wood is almost indestructible,
and in the Middle Ages it was used
to build ships and houses and cathedrals.
Oak bark was used to tan leather, and oak acorns
were food for both animals and people.

European Mistletoe

Viscum album

Mistletoe legends reach back to Norse mythology
and Virgil's *Aeneid*. Mistletoe was the
druids' golden herb.
Robed in white, they cut it with a golden sickle
and caught it in a white cloth
before it touched the ground.
It symbolized purity and strength, and
was hung in houses to bring happiness,
promote romance, and enforce peace. If enemies
met beneath the mistletoe they disarmed and kept
a truce that day. Because of the plant's pagan associations,
the Church banned it from Christmas ceremonies,
but its magic was thought to be so strong
that people used it secretly, and even
monks wore it as a hidden amulet.
It was believed to exorcise witches and demons and to
protect its wearer from fits,
lung fever, tremors, and poison.
European mistletoe grows on oaks.
American mistletoe, of the same family but a
different species, grows on maples and black gum trees.

English Holly

Ilex aquifolium

Holly was known and revered by early British druids
and Roman pagans. The druids thought it was
a special favorite of the sun because it was evergreen.
The Romans used it as a charm to ward off
lightning and evil spells
and believed its blossoms could repel poison.
They sent sprigs of holly to their friends
during Saturnalia, the winter festival
of the god Saturn. The early Christian Church forbade
the use of holly, particularly during Saturnalia,
but the Romans largely ignored the ban.
So did the British, among whom arose the custom
of hanging sprigs of holly about the house
as hiding places for Christmas elves and fairies.
In Germany a soberer legend evolved
about the holly, which was called christdorn,
or Christ's crown of thorns.
The berries were believed to have been white
until they were stained by Christ's blood.

Ivy

Hedera helix

The traditions held holly to be a man's plant,
ivy a woman's. To the Greeks, ivy was an emblem
of happiness and honor.
Poets were crowned with it.
Bacchus, the god of wine, wore a
rather rakish crown of ivy.
Its black berries
at one time were thought to be
a remedy for the plague. They weren't, of course.
Throughout Europe, ivy was used as decoration
for churches and homes at Christmas,
but only for outer passages and on doorways
because of its pagan associations.
It was put up on Christmas Eve and taken down
on the second day of February, Candlemas Eve.
Poles twined with ivy and holly,
the woman's plant and the man's, were set up
for Christmas sports and games.

Laurel

Laurus nobilis

The laurel of the legends is the European species,
not America's laurel-magnolia, also called sweet bay,
or our flowering mountain laurel.
The European laurel was chewed by
the priestesses at Delphi
to inspire visions and prophecies,
and its leaves were burned for incense.
Poets and heroes were crowned with laurel leaves—
we still speak of "winning the laurels"—
and young doctors when they finished their studies
were crowned with laurel at the berry stage.
From this, *bacca* plus *laureus*, came "baccalaureate"
and "bachelor." In later times, after the advent
of Christianity, laurel was used to
decorate churches and houses
at Christmas and in some places in Greece is still
spread on church floors on Holy Saturday.
It is also used as a charm to ward off thunderstorms,
witches, and devils.
We use the leaves, bay leaves, in cooking.

Rosemary

Rosmarinus officinalis

The legends say that, on the flight into Egypt,
Mary was sheltered by a rosemary bush,
and hence rosemary blooms
on the day of Christ's Passion.
So it was long used to decorate
homes and churches at Christmas.
A symbol of remembrance and thus a funeral herb,
it was carried by mourners and planted near graves.
But it was also a token of happiness,
often used in bridal bouquets.
The Romans wove rosemary into garlands
for their guests and for the statues of their gods.
Over the centuries, it has been
a kind of all-purpose herb, elixir,
tonic, and purifier of dreams,
and has even served as incense
in humble country churches.

Christmas Rose

Helleborus niger

Various plants have been called Christmas rose,
but perhaps best known is this black hellebore.
The Christmas rose isn't really a rose at all,
but is related to the buttercup.
It has been used as a medicine
and a poison for thousands of years.
From Egypt it was taken to early Greece
and used to treat epilepsy, gout,
and mental disorders. It was strewn about
the house to dispel evil spirits.
One early legend says a little shepherd girl wept
because she had no gift for the Babe on the night of
the Nativity. An angel took pity on her and,
with a lily for a wand, commanded the *Helleborus niger*,
which grew nearby, to blossom.
It did, for the first time ever,
and the little girl gathered an armful and took them
to the stable in Bethlehem.
She was exalted when the Babe turned from the gifts
of the Magi and reached for the flowers.

19

Poinsettia

Euphorbia pulcherrima

The poinsettia, native to the New World,
is one of the very few strictly American plants
that have been absorbed
into the body of Christmas legends.
It has become a traditional Christmas plant
chiefly because of its bright red color.
But there is a Mexican legend about the poinsettia
that clearly is related to the legend about
hellebore, the Christmas rose.
In this Mexican version, a little girl,
child of a family of poor peasants,
was on her way to church
on Christmas Eve and was so sad
at having no gift to place at the altar
for the Virgin and Child that she wept.
An angel heard and told her to gather
an armload of twigs from the roadside.
She did, and by the time she reached the church
they were in full bloom, an armload of poinsettias,
a beautiful gift to place at the altar.